Random

Thoughts

Chris Corcoran

ACCENT PRESS LTD

Random Thoughts

Published by Accent Press Ltd – 2010

ISBN 9781907016387

The Quick Reads project in Wales is a joint venture between Basic
Skills Cymru and the Welsh Books Council. Titles are funded through
Basic Skills Cymru as part of the National Basic Skills Strategy for
Wales on behalf of the Welsh Assembly Government.

Printed and bound in the UK

Cover design by Zipline Creative Ltd
Cover photos – Darren Warner

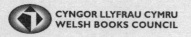

CYNGOR LLYFRAU CYMRU
WELSH BOOKS COUNCIL

Noddir gan
Lywodraeth Cynulliad Cymru
Sponsored by
Welsh Assembly Government

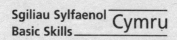

Sgiliau Sylfaenol
Basic Skills _____ **Cymru**

Introduction

Hello, reader. Thanks for picking up this book. If you are reading it because someone gave it to you, I hope you are not too disappointed. If, however, you are reading this book in a bookshop and you're 'umming' and 'ahhhing' about whether to buy it, then for goodness' sake make a snap decision; there's a queue forming behind you. This book is placed at the till for a reason. It is an *impulse buy*. You're not supposed to think about it: you're supposed to chuck it in your basket with your *Harry Potter*. If it's rubbish you've only wasted £1.99.

Well, that's the hard sell over. If you are still reading and you've felt even the hint of a smile, there's a good chance you'll enjoy the rest of this. Go on, take a risk. At the absolute worst you'll have bought an ideal fix for a wobbly coffee table. And at best, you might laugh out loud on a train.

All the best.

Radio Ga Ga

I thought I'd kick off this book with a story from my childhood. As a kid I was a massive Queen fan. I liked their early albums best, *A Night at the Opera*, *A Day at the Races*, *Sheer Heart Attack* and the like. I liked their 80s stuff too, at the time, although looking back it wasn't as good. Being a Queen fan has been a bit like eating an entire tin of Quality Street in one go: amazing at the start, a pleasure but with diminishing returns in the middle and, by the time you reached *Innuendo*, all you were left with was the soft-rock equivalent of the Toffee Penny. I was such a big fan I can remember spending one summer holiday not down the beach in the sun like normal kids, but in record shops in Tenby looking for a Queen T-shirt.

In 1989 I was in the Lower Sixth, which, in my opinion, was the best year in school. You got free lessons on your timetable, there was no real exam pressure and we had a common room with a broken sofa. Our days were spent lounging around, playing cards, flirting and being amused by the mangy terrier that would burst in and destroy the pencil case of anyone dull enough to have left their bag unattended.

This was the time sixth formers started getting wheels. One of my best mates, Paulo, an Italian with a passion for motor racing, had got a car. He wasn't a typical Italian when it came to cars. He used to keep to the speed limit, play Dire Straits and, I'm sure, if it had been as customary in the 80s as it had been in the 50s, he'd have worn a pair of string-back driving gloves. But that didn't matter because for Dan, Sul, The Boy and me, it meant that we had our freedom. All we had to worry about on any one journey was which cassette to play and how often we should sing 'I've got a dog whose name is Rover':

I've got a dog whose name is Rover,
Name is Rover, shits all over,
I've got a dog whose name is Rover – shit, shit, shit.
Shit on the ceiling,
Shit on the floor,
Shit on the window,
Shit on the door,
Shit over here,
Shit over there,

4

Shit everywhere,
SHIT!

We didn't realise it at the time, but apparently we were in the top three per cent of the country intellectually, and it showed!

All around south Wales we went, down the beach, clubbing in Cardiff, off to rugby matches. And we now had access to school parties. The school party – a den of iniquity involving cheap cider, Frankie Goes To Hollywood and clumsy fumbles.

One Friday night we went to a school party in a function room above a workingmen's club somewhere in the Rhymney Valley. It was an excuse to dress up and look your best. For me, that meant grey cords, pink Fred Perry T-shirt, Bros hairdo, a liberal splash of Kouros aftershave (it took longer to get out of the presentation box than it took to shave off my tiny bit of bum-fluff) and grey slip-on shoes. In summary? Slick. It was someone's birthday party, and we'd been told there was going to be a bar and a disco. There was also going to be a girl there I liked.

OK, so there were lots of girls that I liked. In fact, there were very few girls I didn't like. I was a seventeen-year-old sexual firework ready to go off. In fact, 'ready to go off' doesn't do justice to the sort of pent-up energy coursing through my veins. I was a sexual firework who was one spark short of the sort of display that would make the organisers of the 1999 Sydney Harbour Bridge show feel inadequate. And I say *I* liked this girl, but *everyone* liked this girl. She was *the* girl.

Jackie was to a teenage boy what catnip is to a tomcat – for she had curves. Proper curves. Olympic curves. Eighth Wonder of the World curves. 'Is-your-blouse-too-tight-or-have-they-grown-since-this-morning?' curves. When she walked past you in the playground the only thing you could do was to give in to the feeling of hopelessness and try not to make a noise. Not an easy thing to do when you consider that what held these curves in check was a white blouse and a black bra. Yep, she had the three Bs – boobs, blouse and bra. The Holy Trinity. In the language of three-card brag, she held a prial of threes. To use a football term, she was scoring a perpetual hat trick. She made me go all warm and bubbly when I looked at her. The weird thing was that, apparently, she liked me.

We arrived at the club and as Paulo put on his crook lock, Dan, The Boy, Sul and I went inside. We walked up the narrow staircase to the function room, past the adverts for 'Singing Star, Danny Star – Sings' and reminders for members to pay their £1 subs. When we opened the door, there she was, right by the bar.

'There she is,' grinned Dan, 'right there by the bar.' His deep voice carried his statement of the obvious within earshot. He had a voice that didn't really match the way he looked – like a small, skinny prisoner of war from World War Two.

'Oh yeah, good work, Dan. Why don't you just go over and say, "Hey, my mate likes you"?'

'Do you want me to?'

'Very funny. Sush.'

''Cos I will if you want me to.' He grinned.

'Look, shut up. What you drinking?'

'Lager, please.'

I turned to The Boy and Sul. 'Boys?'

'Lager,' said The Boy.

Sul added, 'And a Snowball for Nigel Mansell.'

'Three pints of lager and an orange juice please,' I said to the bar-child.

'We've only got Kronenbourg 1664. Is that all right?' she squeaked.

Now there are certain points in your life when you say 'yes' when you should have said

7

'no'. In hindsight, this was one of them. I didn't know how strong Kronenbourg was.

'Yes, that's fine,' I said. I needed a drink quick to control the bitter-sweet adrenalin of having been within inches of Jackie, who was wearing some sort of jaw-dropping see-through top and wafting out some intoxicating girl smell. The second half of the same drink would be used to calm the now rising panic caused by her having gone to sit down with her mates across the other side of the room. Still: be cool, I thought. It's a marathon, not a sprint, and at least she's away from Dan.

'Cheers,' said Dan as I gave him his pint. He set off in her direction.

I managed to avoid catastrophe by scooping him up and going to dance to The Pogues' 'Fiesta'. In fairness, what Dan was doing, and later what The Boy and Sul did (having the DJ dedicate, on my behalf, Motörhead's 'The Ace Of Spades' 'to a special little lady in the room') was just good-natured high jinks.

Paulo nearly messed up the whole night by saying he wanted to go home early because he was tired. Actually, kids were playing football in the car park and he was worried about his wing mirrors. So we ignored him. We all settled into the night, and like a coiled spring I kept my eye on Jackie and waited for my moment to strike. Sorry, not a coiled spring. I mean a cobra. Actually a cobra sounds a bit aggressive. Let's just say I waited for the moment I could go and speak to Jackie.

But the moment didn't come. As the night moved on, she didn't. She stayed sitting with her mates and only ventured on to the dance floor twice: once for Wham!'s 'Freedom' and the other for Duran Duran's 'Rio'. On neither occasion was she alone. Every now and then she'd look over and give me hope, but she never once left the safety of the herd. It was infuriating. With no solution to hand I did what most blokes my age would have done in the 80s. I gave up and resigned myself to an evening of drinking, ironic break-dancing and synchronised Status Quo air guitar. By a quarter past ten I stood at the bar a little frustrated and more than a little drunk.

But then something happened that only happens in films. And like in films, it all happened in slow-mo. I don't know how much time had passed, but all of a sudden she was on her own.

How did that happen? I thought, and then realised I didn't know and it didn't matter. The key was to act. Just as I started to think about how I was going to get to sit down next to her, she gestured for me to sit down next to her.

Shit, I thought. I'm in! Now take a deep breath and be cool.

I suddenly sobered up and walked over as coolly as possible. This meant that I did a sort of stupid show biz sideways walk down the three steps from the bar to the edge of the dance floor, like celebrities do when they're on *Parkinson*. But she didn't mind! In fact, she found it funny! And to show her appreciation, as soon as I came into range, she grabbed my hand, sat me down and put my arm around her neck. I couldn't believe what was happening. It was like a Richard Curtis film before Richard Curtis films had been invented.

I was seconds away from kissing Jackie, the goddess of the school, and as yet I hadn't had to *do* anything. This was, beyond question, the highlight of my life. In fact, so shocked was my fatalistic side that it had already sent a quick prayer up to God asking him to take me now, as life could only go downhill from here. Luckily, my optimistic side gestured to the see-through blouse and pointed out that this could merely be the *start* of many *more* moments such as these. My fatalistic side saw the point, retracted the celestial request and then passed out.

The trouble was, by this time I had drunk six pints of Kronenbourg.

Normally, if you'd reached this point in the game, being a bit pissed didn't matter. You didn't need your legs. Your body could shut down all limbs and put all its attention on your tongue and your Lothario eyebrow. But this was *strong* lager. Stronger than I realised and it affected me in such an unpredictable way that even as I write this now twenty years on I still can't believe what happened next.

Just as Jackie began to turn her head towards me, a head turn that would inevitably end in her giving me the look of permission, 'Radio Ga Ga' came on.

Now, on paper, the choice between 'kiss goddess' or 'get up and do "Radio Ga Ga" on dance floor alone' is a no-brainer. No matter how big a Queen fan you are, you'd select the former. Yep, just checking. No-brainer. But for me, at that moment, the scenario that promised the best reward seemed to be the latter. Like Pavlov's dog I was up, out of my seat, and on the dance floor in one quick Freddie Mercury snake-hips stride.

This was the happiest I had ever felt.

'I feel so alive!' I screamed gaily in my head.

'All we hear is...' I sang, my arms spread wide like a soccer hooligan, 'Radio Ga Ga...'

Oh, this is great, I thought. If she liked my *Parkinson* walk she'll be loving this!

'Radio Goo Goo...' Kronenbourg sloshed around my brain, mixing my emotions with my political sympathies.

What a great film *Metropolis* was, I thought. It so perfectly summed up the industrialisation of labour. How clever to use it in a rock video!

'Radio Ga Ga...' I closed my eyes.

This, my friends, is Utopia! I thought. I was doing the best impression of the best video of all time and Jackie the school goddess was on the back burner.

There was my mistake, right there. The words 'goddess' and 'back burner' don't go together. Girls don't *wait*.

When I opened my eyes I saw my mates. I frowned. Paulo and Sul looked like they'd seen a ghost and The Boy had his head in his hands. Bucking the trend was Dan who stood with his arms aloft as though he had just won the World Cup. I turned around, like a voyeur rubbernecking a car crash, to where Jackie had been sitting. She had gone.

By the time I turned back, my mates had joined me on the dance floor.

'What the fuck are you doing?' said Paulo. It was the first time he had ever sworn.

'I don't know,' I said.

'Well done,' said The Boy. 'The best example of pulling defeat from the jaws of victory I've ever seen.'

'Bollocks!' I said.

'You twat,' said Sul.

'... radio what's new?' sang Dan.

'... Radio!' he continued with the others joining in, laughing.

'Some...

one...

still...

loves...

yoooooooooou...'

Years later Dan told me that he'd had the DJ put 'Radio Ga Ga' on deliberately just to see what I would do. He had bet Sul I would get up. Sul had bet I would stay put. Sul lost a pound. Bastard!

What Are We Like?

We live in the 21st century and any attempt at describing national character often leads to clumsy stereotypes, but I think it is fair to say that nationalities have traits. One that I think Welsh people have is an innocent naivety.

I used to teach in Barry Boys School and one day I took some of the Certificate of Education Group on a day trip to Pontypridd to see an ex-mining area. These were the sort of kids most people saw as too much trouble. As one senior member of staff said to me at the time, 'You're taking that lot to Pontypridd? You're a braver man than me. I wouldn't take them to the end of the drive.' We had a great day. We saw terraced houses, we saw old mine shafts, we had a cup of tea in an Italian Bracchi café and just before we left, one of the boys had a piss in the multi-storey. All fairly standard. On the way home, a journey of less than thirty minutes, all the boys dropped off to sleep. One of them woke up and said, with wonder and awe in his voice, 'Whoa, boys, just think: twenty minutes ago we were in Ponty!'

It was a genuinely touching moment. A few of them, though fifteen years old, hadn't ever been out of Barry. If they had just been on a day trip to NASA and one of them had woken up and said, 'Whoa, boys, just think: twenty minutes ago we were in outer space!' it would have been no more mind-blowing to them.

I witnessed an adult version of this sort of naivety when I was in Paris for the Six Nations. An old boy who looked like he'd never been out of Merthyr before, never mind on a rugby tour, stumbled, drunk, out of a strip club. He stopped on the pavement, his eyes wide in awe. He looked like he'd just seen the meaning of life, and it turned out it had nothing to do with what he'd been taught at chapel. Gesturing with his thumb back over his shoulder he said, 'What the bloody hell's going on in there?' Then after a split second of reflection he said, 'I'm going back in.'

This sort of naivety is a nice characteristic, I think. It reflects intrinsic warmth about us as a people.

Another trait I think we have is honesty. I will now outline a conversation I had with a decorator who was doing my house while I was away on tour. I had dialled his number. There was a long ring and eventually he answered, 'Hello?'

'Hello,' I said. 'Byron?'

'Yes.'

'It's Chris.'

'Who?'

'Chris.'

'Chris who?'

'Chris Corcoran. You're standing in my lounge.'

'Oh, hiya, Chris, all right, boy?'

'Yeah I'm good. How's it looking?'

'What?'

'The lounge.'

'Er... not that great.'

'Really? How do you mean?'

'Well, I'd probably best describe it as nearly OK.'

'Oh,' I said, 'that's no good. I want it to be, you know, "wow", "amazing"!'

'Oh, it's not that,' he said.

'OK,' I said, 'just describe to me what "nearly OK" looks like.'

There was a long pause.

'Er...' he said eventually, '... well, if you're far enough away, you can't see the streaks!'

'Byron,' I said, 'are you saying that every time I want to use the lounge from now on, in order that my eyes are not offended, I'm going to have to sit in the middle of my room, equidistant from the walls?'

'Oh, yeah,' he said, all upbeat, 'if you do that it'll be fine.'

By this stage I was amused, actually enjoying myself. But the best was yet to come.

'Byron,' I said, and I admit I knew that the mild sarcasm to follow would bounce right back at me, unregistered, 'if I'm going to sacrifice the use of 98% of my lounge, it can't be "fine". It'd have to be "spectacular".'

'Oh, it's not that,' he said.

'All right,' I said, realising that he had clearly, somehow, cocked the whole job up, 'do you want to stop doing it?'

'What do you mean now?'

'Do you want to stop painting my lounge? You know, I'll pay you off, like.'

'Oh, really? Can you do that?' he said, delighted. 'That'd be great.'

'Yes,' I said, 'no problem. How much do I owe you?'

'Oh,' he said, clearly relieved. 'Let's just call it building materials.'

'Really? You don't want anything for your labour?'

'No,' he said. 'I've made a right pig's ear of this. To be honest, it looked better before I started.'

At which point I laughed and said, 'OK, leave an invoice on the window-sill.'

'All right, thanks, Chris,' he said.

'Hey, Byron,' I said. 'Don't take this the wrong way, but why are you a decorator if you're so bad at it?'

'I'm not a decorator,' he said. 'I'm a plumber. I hate decorating. I don't know one end of a paintbrush from another.'

'That explains it,' I said.

'Eh, listen,' he said as though he was letting me in on a secret, 'if ever you need any plumbing done give me a shout. You got my number. I'm all right at that.'

'Will do,' I said, 'thanks. Ta-ra.'

'Ta-ra, boy.'

Luckily as yet I've not had a leak.

Gulliver's Desserts

I was having a sleep on the sofa the other day after a delicious Sunday lunch when my girlfriend woke me up to give me a tub of Petits Filous and for a split second I thought I'd become a giant. I hadn't of course. I'd just been given a tiny yogurt that made my hand look massive.

It's not enough of anything to be called a dessert, is it? As a dessert experience it's almost pointless. On the side it says 'Little Pots of Fun'. That's not a pot. You plant flowers in a pot. Pots are quite big. There's a phrase, 'I haven't got a pot to piss in.' You couldn't piss in that. It'd be full in no time. Also, you can't describe eating a Petits Filous as 'fun' because it's over too quick. Surely 'fun' equals 'stimulus' plus 'time'? Ten-pin bowling is fun but if you only did it for two seconds, which is the average time it takes to eat a Petits Filous, it would be a pretty disappointing night out. Eating a Petits Filous is over so quickly it is, at best, briefly pleasant. It is the yogurt equivalent of a sneeze.

The only reason this is an issue for me is that after I had finished it I asked my girlfriend if I could have another one, but was accused of being greedy.

'You can't have *two* pots,' she said.

'But they are tiny,' I said.

'It doesn't matter,' she said. 'It's still two.'

'Yes,' I said, 'but if I eat two there's a chance I'll have some fun, which is, after all, what they are advertising on the side of the pot.'

'What?' she called from the kitchen.

'It's just occurred to me that "fun" equals "stimulus" plus "time".'

'What are you talking about?' She was being very tolerant.

'If I eat two Petits Filous that will be at least four seconds of yogurt experience and while not quite the same as doing a skydive, at least I'd be heading in the "fun" direction.'

She poked her head into the lounge.

'No, it's still *two*. Now come in here, Einstein, and help me with the dishes.' Fair enough, I thought. My only contribution to lunch preparation had been laying the table, so this was an entirely reasonable request. The last thing you need in the aftermath of a Sunday roast is someone reflecting on a mathematical concept of 'fun' instead of picking up a dishcloth.

However, since then, I have come to a conclusion on whether eating two Petits Filous is greedy. To eat two doughnuts *is* greedy. To eat two *normal* yogurts is greedy too, maybe, but two Petits Filous? No. Eating two Petits Filous is not greedy. It's OK. Boys, I know that girlfriends are nearly always right and by listening to them we benefit greatly, but there comes a time when you need to make a stand. You may get the shit kicked out of you, but sometimes you just have to make a stand.

Girls, I would like to stress this applies only to Petits Filous. Nothing else.

Camping Holidays and Snowdon

I went camping recently to Snowdon. It was fantastic. I think camping is as close to becoming a hunter-gatherer as a townie can get. Obviously, these days you only have to hunt as far as the local Co-op and gather stuff off the shelves, but the rest of the time it's just you versus the elements. Well, you versus the elements but with access to a block of reliable showers, an amazing tent, a car, and a nearby Jamie Oliver gastro-pub.

The fact is that camping is a lot easier than it used to be. These days everything does everything itself. I have got a tent that puts itself up. It's brilliant. You just pull it out of its case and it springs up in a second. Mind you, getting it back in at the end of the holiday is totally impossible as, having enjoyed its freedom, it is less 'willing-camping-companion' and more 'resentful-genie'. Nonetheless, it is instant camping and easily beats the tedious hours of putting together a scout-troop-special with half the poles missing.

A self-erecting tent is pretty amazing, but the other mind-boggling invention you can now get is self-heating food. No cooker or pan of hot water needed, nothing. You just twist the packet to release a chemical reaction that heats the food. I'm more sceptical about this invention. I mean, imagine explaining it to your granny. Back in her day, they'd have run you out of town for witchcraft – the idea of pickling was the devil's work. Still, it is an unbelievable invention, perfect for the 80s generation who are used to popping bubble wrap.

But, however much easier camping now is, it is still a return to the simple pleasures of life, one of which is how much better food tastes when you are standing in a field. Shreddies, for example, go from being a simple cereal to a malted breakfast experience. Never has the combination of creamy milk and crunchy, malty, soggy latticey cereal been so delicious. As for biscuits, you can keep luxury offerings like Hazelnut Boasters and Viscount Mint Creams: a Bourbon in a field is the greatest. If you get migraines or panic attacks don't, whatever you do, eat cheese in a field. I had a piece of mild Cheddar while making some sandwiches for lunch and so strong was the flavour I had to go and have a lie-down. Now, I don't know why flavour is so much better in a field, but I am sure scientists could prove it if they tried. Maybe when you're out in the fresh air, your hunter-gatherer mode kicks in and your taste buds up their game to inspire you to go out and get food. Obviously if your survival instinct continues to evolve, one day it would put less emphasis on exaggerating your taste and more on exaggerating the urge to go out and collect Tesco Club Card points. But, so amazing is the experience of eating outside, that I have come to the conclusion that there is little that could not be resolved sitting in a field over a risotto. I reckon if you sat Presidents Obama, Medvedev, Ahmadinejad and Kim Jong-il down in a field, and had Nelson Mandela serve them up a bacon risotto in a plastic bowl, you could actually achieve world peace.

This holiday wasn't just spent standing in a field marvelling at the previously unnoticed flavour of cucumber. It was active, too, and on one day we walked up Snowdon. Now, before I tell you what happened, consider this. Have you ever noticed, when you watch the London Marathon, just how many people are in it who shouldn't be? I reckon at least a quarter of the people who line up at the start each year have given no thought as to what they are about to do. You can't run twenty-six miles if the longest walk you've done over the last sixteen years is to the treat tin. Wearing long shorts may stop your fat thighs rubbing together, but it won't stop you getting a heart attack. Nor will blind optimism, carrying a bucket, or dressing up as Scooby Do. In fact, I think you should only be able to ask someone for sponsorship for the London Marathon if you accurately describe what you will be doing. So, everyone who has done a six-month training programme could fairly claim to be 'running the marathon, for a good cause'. People who haven't completed such a programme should have to say they will be 'taking up vital NHS resources through stupidity, for a good cause' and everyone else should be forced to say they are 'probably going to die for a good cause'.

Well, the same thing applies to climbing mountains.

To walk up and back down Snowdon takes about five hours, and it's hard going, yet my trip up Snowdon was like an *I Spy* of 'people you wouldn't expect to see on a mountain'. I saw grannies walking at about one mile an hour talking about whist-drives, I saw a man in wellies, a group of Goths, some girls who looked like they'd got terribly lost on the way to a nightclub, a stag-night party dressed as superheroes, a Sikh family dressed for a wedding, a hippy coming down the mountain in a pair of clogs, a toddler with a bike (yes, a bike!) and a very camp man wearing a vest and shorts carrying an empty grocery bag going *up* the mountain at a quarter to five! Where was he going? God only knows, although it was a journey that was surely to end in disappointment, as what there definitely *isn't* at the top of Snowdon is a late-night Waitrose. However, all of the above were like Sir Ranulph Fiennes compared to poor old Brenda.

Brenda was an eighteen-stone mother-of-three who was trying to walk up Snowdon in flip-flops. She was so sunburned that at first glance I thought she was a post box. I know her name was Brenda because her impatient family was about fifty yards higher up shouting stuff like, 'it's not far, Brenda', 'little bit further', 'you're nearly there'. The trouble was, Brenda was far from 'nearly there' as what lay ahead of her wasn't 'a little bit further', it was bloody miles! It was an hour's vertical climb for a person of average fitness, so for Brenda? Probably two days. What Brenda *needed* was not to 'be brave' but a helicopter.

'Come on, Brenda, what are you doing?' said her husband up ahead. He was big and hard-looking. In fact they all were. They were the sort of family that on a Bank Holiday would sit in a beer garden drinking cider, shouting at their dog and letting their kids eat soil.

'Just having a bit of a rest,' she said. She wasn't. She was stuck on the side of a mountain. The London Marathon theory of blind optimism wasn't working, although I've no doubt that if her husband *had* been carrying a Wonder Woman outfit and a fund-raising bucket, he'd have offered them as a solution. As I drew nearer, I realised that, actually, this was quite a serious situation. Despite being out of date by ten years my Bronze Medallion Life-saving instincts kicked in. Brenda was in trouble and she needed to get down. The trouble was she was going to struggle to do this on her own, so there was a chance the mountain rescue was going to be needed. This was: a) likely to be unpopular with Brenda as it would be embarrassing, and b) likely to be unpopular with her family as it would almost certainly mean the end of their walk. Worst of all, my role in this was going to be that of know-it-all interfering stranger and about as popular as a fox with a napkin at the Chicken & Goose Ball. All I knew was that I had to say something and it had to be so tactful and so perceptive that it would defuse a difficult domestic situation and help rescue a woman from mortal danger. It had to combine charm and common sense while at the same time offer a practical solution.

Excuse me, are you in trouble? No good, I thought; might cause panic.

Hiya, this mountain bit bigger than you thought, is it? Not bad, but suggested stupidity. This was a woman who had just discovered her physical limitations. The last thing she needed was someone pointing out her mental ones.

Hello, you look like someone who's regretting eating too many crisps. This wasn't going well. Before I knew it, I'd drawn level with her. It was now or never.

'All right? How's it going?' I said. Genius! A woman's life hangs in the balance, and that's the best I could come up with?

'Just having a bit of a rest,' she said. 'Is it far to the top, do you know?'

'Well…' I said.

Say yes, I thought.

'… um… well…'

Say 'yes, I do know, Brenda, it's bloody miles…'

'… it's… um…'

Say it! Say '… it's bloody miles, Brenda, stop this madness…'

'… well… it's…'

Say 'it's bloody miles, Brenda, stop this madness and for the love of God SAVE YOURSELF AND GET OFF THIS BLOODY MOUNTAIN, YOU BIG FLIP-FLOP MENTALIST!'

'… it's…'

'For Christ's sake, Brenda, hurry up,' shouted her husband as he sparked open a can of Foster's that sprayed over the bull-dog tattoo on his chest.

'… it's not far, Brenda,' I said. 'Little bit further, you're nearly there.'

I felt a bit guilty, obviously, but as I sat around the camp-fire that night, sipping the most beery-tasting beer I'd ever had, I comforted myself with the thought that by avoiding a potential confrontation with Brenda's husband what I had actually done was applied the first lesson of Life-saving, which is 'never put yourself in danger'. As I lay down that night I realised that since I hadn't heard a helicopter fly over, Brenda had clearly got down fine. I had done the right thing. And then I heard a helicopter fly over.

Dragon Cabs

One of the main taxi firms in Cardiff is Dragon Cabs and every time I call them I can't help but think how great it would be if what actually came to pick you up was an actual dragon. Better still, if dragons were just part of a fleet of mythical creatures. Be great, wouldn't it, to be standing amongst the three-in-the-morning, town-centre carnage of an international rugby day and overhear…

'Hello?'

'Hello, Dragon Cabs.'

'Hiya, can I book a dragon please?'

'Where you travelling to?'

(TO HIS MATES) 'Boys, where we going?' (TURNS BACK TO PHONE) 'Aberdare, but there's five of us.'

'Dragons are only licensed for four.'

'Yes, please.'

'Sorry?'

'What? Sorry, it's a bit noisy here.'

'I said a dragon is only licensed for four.'

'Oh right, hang on.' (TO HIS MATES)

31

'Dragons can only take four, boys.'

'What you on about? They're massive!'

'Aye, but they've only got a licence for four.'

'Bollocks, tell her Dai can sit on its neck.'

(TURNS BACK TO PHONE) 'Hello.'

'Hello?'

'One of my mates is only five foot two, can he just sit on its neck?'

'No.'

(TO HIS MATES) 'She won't do it.'

'Ask her why.'

(TURNS BACK TO PHONE) 'Sorry, hope you don't mind me asking, why not?'

'It's where the magic scales are.'

(TO HIS MATES) 'It's where the magic scales are.'

'Oh fair enough, what else they got?'

'Hiya…'

'I've got a Minotaur, he takes five but he can't come for an hour. He's doing a hen do in Tredegar.'

'Oh, we need to go now, really.'

'How about three phoenixes?'

'No, too expensive.'

'A unicorn?'

'Will he definitely come?'

'No guarantee he will, nor that he even exists.'

'Oh.'

'Well, in that case, all I've got left are single-seater orcs.'

(TO HIS MATES) 'All she's got is orcs.'

'Oh for fu–!'

(TURNS BACK TO PHONE) 'That's piggy-back only, is it?'

'Yes and no guarantee they'll take you to where you want to go, but they can be there in two minutes.'

'OK, hang on.'

(TO HIS MATES) 'She says all she's got left is orcs, piggy-back only and no guarantee he'll take you home but they'll be here now.'

(PAUSE/MOUTHFUL) 'Ask her can we eat our kebabs while we travel.'

'Can we eat while we travel?'

'Yes, you can't make them smell any worse than they already do.'

(TO HIS MATES) 'Yes. She says they stink like shit.'

'Tidy.'

Don't suppose I'll see it in my lifetime, but be good, eh?

Doodle Do's and Doodle Don'ts

When doing kids' telly you have to be careful what you say. For example, you have to say 'sticky tape' instead of Sellotape and 'glue stick' instead of Pritt Stick as these are brand names, and on the BBC you can't advertise. Until I got the hang of this on *Doodle Do* we did numerous retakes of perfectly good scenes because I had said the wrong thing. One of the weirdest things, however, is what you can't say or do because of health and safety. For example, you can't use scissors or lick stuff or violently poke a child in the eye with a paintbrush. (Don't ask me how the latter happened. It wasn't nearly as funny as I thought it was going to be, and I have since apologised.)

There were two restrictions that I had to enforce during recording that, when I was first told, I genuinely thought were a wind-up. The first was a health and safety issue associated with the advanced *Doodle Do* art project, 'Parrot Skittles'. If you haven't had the pleasure of watching a man whose only artistic qualification is a B grade at GCSE create a Parrot Skittle, I shall explain how it's done. What you need is a toilet roll, some colourful paint, some glue, some stickers, some feathers from an art shop (not from a pet) and a paintbrush. What you do is mix the paint with the glue, which you then paint on to the toilet roll. Then you stick the stickers on as eyes and a beak and then you cover your parrot in feathers. Once you have repeated this nine times and let them all dry, all you have to do is find a tennis ball for the hours of fun to begin.*

Right, pop quiz! Who can spot the health and safety issue here? Hmm, tricky isn't it? There isn't a lot there to put a child in danger, is there? Don't drink glue? Don't pour paint into your eyes? Don't try to stick feathers on a real parrot? All of these could indeed be seen as health and safety hazards, but are clearly too ridiculous to mention. But the issue that we had to deal with was equally ludicrous and it was as follows: we weren't allowed to say the phrase 'toilet roll'. More to the point, we weren't allowed to *use* a toilet roll.

But wasn't the body of the parrot *made* out of a toilet roll? Was not the parrot *without* a

---

* Two to three minutes of kids trying to knock down skittles before getting bored and then pestering you to put *Shrek* on.

toilet roll merely a pile of gluey feathers with a face like the creature from the *Goonies*? In fact, couldn't you even claim that this art project was 'toilet-roll reliant'? All questions that I asked and to which the answer is of course 'yes'. Nonetheless, I was told what we had to use was something that looked exactly like a toilet roll, and had all the qualities of a toilet roll, but wasn't actually a toilet roll. What we needed was a toilet roll substitute, and what we used was half a tinfoil cardboard tube.

'But doesn't a tinfoil cardboard tube ripped in half leave your parrot with a *ripped head*?' I remember asking. 'Especially if we can't straighten him up with a pair of scissors?'

'Well, yes it does,' I was told.

'So why can't we just use a toilet roll?'

'Just in case it encourages kids to go rooting around in toilets.'

That was the reason.

'Are you serious?' I said, looking around for people laughing, but there were none.

'Yes, it's health and safety.'

How ridiculous is that? Isn't finding out where the toilet is all part of toilet training? Surely familiarity with the location of the bog reduces the chances of kids having a crap in the lounge. I mean, what's the worst that can happen? A kid mistakes the toilet for a swimming pool and gets in? I remember doing that as a kid and all that happened to me was that my feet got wet. My parents didn't sue the local baths!

I suppose there is a small chance it could be a bit unhygienic, but is it any less of a threat than encouraging them to go and get a cardboard tube from a box with a serrated edge? If you keep your tinfoil where I keep mine, it's in the knife drawer. Frankly, if I was six, I'd rather take my chances with a bog brush than half a dozen Kitchen Devils in a drawer just above eye level.

Similarly, the last thing you want is for them to start confusing the tinfoil for toilet paper. If there is one thing about tinfoil of which there is no doubt, it's that it isn't very absorbent.

When it comes to health and safety, clearly the world has gone mad. I once saw an almond tart in the BBC canteen labelled as 'contains nuts'. Has it really come to this? If everyone is viewed as deeply stupid then *everything* is potentially dangerous. You could probably kill yourself brushing your teeth if you were stupid enough, but do we really need to label a toothbrush as a choking hazard? I imagine you could do a fair amount of damage if you shoved a pencil in your ear, but is a public information film really the answer? There's a slim chance you could rupture an artery with nail clippers if you slipped violently enough, but should the nail clipper industry post a leaflet through everyone's letterbox to cover themselves? This is insane. Can we please all stop suing each other for five minutes so a kid can find a toilet roll and make a parrot?

The other restriction that made me laugh was when we embarked upon the art project 'Seaside Collage'. In the show that went to air we played a video clip of kids on a beach making a collage of the seaside out of stuff they found there. So they had little pebble boats and seaweed trees and sand for the beach and blue shells for the water. But when it came to doing it in the studio we didn't have anything from the beach. It was all art stuff like tissue paper and towels and egg boxes, although we did have pebbles. When I asked why we didn't have any objects from the beach, I was told it was because it is illegal to take anything from the beach since it belongs to the Queen or the council or Neptune or someone.

'But how come we've got real pebbles?'

'We buy them from the Garden Centre,' they said and I was handed a net bag of pebbles. I was told that when we recorded the take that's what I had to say. I had to tell kids that the place you get pebbles from is the Garden Centre. Not the beach. Only in this consumerist age could that sentence even begin to make sense! Now I'm all for DEFRA introducing a law that prevents illegal dredging or unethical corporations digging up half a beach for use in the building trade, but surely this doesn't apply to a kid with a bucket, does it? Well, apparently it does. The law says that *anyone* taking *anything* from a beach could be prosecuted.

''Ere, you. Where you taking that pebble?'

'I'm six.'

'Put your bucket down and move away from the pebble.'

'You're funny.'

'I'm going to ask you once more to put that pebble back on the beach.'

'I'm going to make a collage. I saw it on *Doodle D…*'

'Right, that's it, get in the back of the van. I'm arresting you on suspicion of pebble theft.'

We live in a world where that actually *could*

happen. Isn't that a bit weird? It can be illegal for a child to take a pebble from a beach but not for a multi-millionaire to have an off-shore bank account. Sorry, is it me, or has there been a mistake?

TV Adverts

Auditions for TV adverts are horrendous. The drill is to walk into the audition studios, fill in a load of forms confirming you are able to do the things your agent lied that you could do, then try to learn something that would normally take you a day in about five minutes. Then, when called, you go into a bare studio and humiliate yourself. The day I decided to stop was at an audition on the hottest day of the year, a few years ago.

The advert was for the new VW Passat. The story of the advert was: posh bloke turns up to expensive hotel in new VW Passat and throws keys to the two doormen dressed in fine attire. They then fight for the privilege to park it. One of them wins and parks it.

As I waited to go in I noticed that people were being called in twos. When it was my turn I got called in with a bloke called Steve, who was a short, stocky, hobbity-type fellow and a total stranger to me. Ah, I thought, we're going to have to improvise an argument.

However, on entering the room, which had no air conditioning and was easily 35 degrees, we were given a set of elbow and knee-pads, the like of which BMX riders would wear, and told to stand next to each other. That's a bit weird, I thought to myself. I thought the characters were posh doormen. What the hell are they doing wearing elbow... And then it dawned on me. It dawned on Steve, too. We looked at each other with doom in our eyes. We hadn't even said 'hello'.

'Right, you'll be aware of the scene,' said the director. 'Basically what we need to see is you two having a fight.'

And that's what happened. I, a grown man who used to be Head of a History Department in a comprehensive school, wrestled with another grown man on the floor of a Soho sauna. We thrashed around for about ten seconds, I got him in a head-lock, he grabbed my leg, we both fell heavily to the floor, one of my knee-pads slid down to my shin, we both blurted out brilliantly improvised stuff like 'no, I want to park it' and eventually we stopped, soaked in sweat. I could tell Steve was thinking the same as me. *Thank God that's over.*

'OK, thank you,' said the director. 'Um, that

42

wasn't very convincing. Can you do it again? This time go for it a bit more.'

What? I thought, as I struggled to reposition my knee-pad with my sweaty fingers. No. No, I can't. Thank you for the opportunity but I feel that perhaps this role is not for me. I would like to withdraw. That's what I should have said because this was one of the periods in my life where I wasn't very fit and Steve the hobbit was a lot stronger than I had anticipated. As I stood there listening to the director (or rather, in my eyes now, the git in glasses), I realised I was exhausted. I hadn't even been able to reposition my knee-pad without hitching up my trouser leg, which now sat pathetically halfway up my calf, revealing a somewhat self-conscious sock.

'Great, off you go, in your own time.'

Something had happened to Steve since our last tussle. He either really wanted this job or he really wanted for it all to end, because he hurled himself at me with a vigour that brought me crashing to the floor.

'Hang on, I wasn't ready!' I said. How old had I become? *Nine??*

'This is great,' said the git in glasses. 'Better.'

Oh, God, I thought, as the hobbit was on top of me trying to pin me down, I'm in trouble here. I know what you're thinking, why didn't I just lie there passively and allow Steve to win? I don't know, but I think it was because I could tell the red mist had fallen over Steve's eyes, and I couldn't take the risk that in the time it took for everyone to realise that I had given up he might actually kill me. If there was one way I knew I didn't want to be found dead, it was wrestling with a man on a floor in Soho.

'Yes, better, and a bit more from you, Chris?' mewed the git as though he was directing *Hamlet*.

I remember thinking that somehow I needed to make this stop and so, with an open fist, I punched Steve in the chin. In his split second of shock, I managed to shove him off me and give him a wedgie.

'Aaaaaaannnnnd stop,' said the git. 'Lovely, thank you very much, gentlemen.'

At last the most humiliating moment of my life had been brought to a close. I couldn't move. I was drenched in sweat and so tired that I needed help to take off my elbow pads, like a toddler needs help to take off his arm bands. To his credit it was Steve, boxer shorts up around his tummy like an American rapper, who obliged.

'Thank you, gents, we'll let you know,' said the git, gesturing us to the door. As we stepped into the bath of heat that was outside, Steve and I shook hands.

'Let us never speak of this to anyone,' said Steve, like the hero from a film.

'OK,' I said. 'May God go with you.'

Sorry, Steve, it's been a long time. I hope you have moved on, as I have. I felt it was my duty to warn others who might venture into a similar situation. I hope you don't mind.

The Alternative Stag Do

When you get to your thirties, stag do's are a pain in the arse. Well, stag do's of *excess* are a pain in the arse. I've never been a great drinker. I was always the first at the Rugby Club Dinner to be sitting in the corner puking into a mop bucket with my trousers round my ankles. As such, over the years, I've always found occasions where there are groups of lads and peer pressure to drink a bit of a challenge. When you're twenty it's fine because even if you're rubbish at it, drinking is exciting and can lead to adventures. I'm pretty sure that the time I ran naked along Swansea sea-front with a cone on my head, or indeed the time I ended up in bed with Miss Dee-Dee DeVille and her lesbian lover Knockers McGee after a London Burlesque Night, wouldn't have happened if I hadn't had a few beers.*

When you get to your thirties, however, you don't really need any artificial team

* One of these events didn't happen.

46

bonding, and you're not affected by peer pressure like you used to be. In fact, when you're in your thirties, classic rules such as 'eating's cheating' and 'no sleep on tour' just make you grouchy. The fact is, the human body needs food. If you don't give it food it gets tired and there is no fun in that. It doesn't matter if you *are* dressed as Popeye or sporting Borat's lime-green Mankini. Not being able to eat food really annoys people. The human body also needs sleep. If you don't let it sleep it gets tired and, again, there is no fun in that. It doesn't matter how many After-Shocks or Vodka Red Bulls you force it to consume, not being able to sleep pisses people off. Peer pressure in your thirties just leads to the ridiculous situation of people buying you beer and you hiding it under your chair until, as happened to me on my last stag do, you find yourself sitting in a shrine to unwanted Guinness.

The other problem with stag do's in your thirties is that you are far less able to tolerate the group idiot. By the time you get to your thirties, you know who in your group of friends is OK and who is an idiot. In fact, if you're lucky, you've got shot of the idiots and are left only with people you like. The problem with the stag do is that, for one weekend only, often abroad, it throws into the mix the peer group wildcard, such as the groom's cousin, who performs soccer chants while checking in to the hotel, or the bride's brother who, instead of speaking to girls, spends the weekend pinching their nipples. It's bad enough just having to tolerate such an addition, but the problem on a stag do is that the least evolved human being seems to set the agenda. Everyone is forced to dumb down to the worst behaviour. The idiot becomes the leader and you, essentially, become the parent of a hyperactive child, the only difference being that, unlike an actual parent of a hyperactive child, you can't force it to take Ritalin.

The result is a weekend where the only thing you consume is booze, you don't sleep, your days blend into nights and the only cultural interaction you have is with a Romanian 'street performer' keen for you to take advantage of her very generous offer of 'bum-sex, cheap bum-sex'. By the time you get home you are completely destroyed and when asked, 'Did you have a nice time?' by your girlfriend, you are forced to say, 'No,' holding out your shaking hands, 'I had a terrible time, look at my hands. My skin has died, I feel sick and, worst of all, I can't remember a thing!'

The time has come, dear reader, to go on record to say that I, Chris Corcoran, no longer want to go on stag weekends where the only thing you bring home is a hospital wristband and an STD from a fountain in Zagreb. What is outlined below is a manifesto for change. It is the stag do that over-thirties would all *like* to go on but are not brave enough to suggest. If you have access to 'Sprach Zarathustra' (the theme from the film *2001: A Space Odyssey*) then put it on now, stand tall and proud and read what is written below out loud, for this is a proposal for The Alternative Stag Do.

I would like to go on a stag do where eating *isn't* cheating. On the contrary, each day starts with a healthy continental breakfast where a round of fruit smoothies must be *downed* at an agreeable rate decided by the individual.

Where the only *throwing up* is of a ball on the tennis lawn, the only *shots* are shared in the billiard room and there is *plenty* of sleep on tour. Where saying the words 'Pinot Grigio', 'Elevenses' or 'a basket of croissants' doesn't make you gay.

Where, after dinner, instead of drinking games, we establish once and for all, through reasoned debate, what the hell it is that Fuzzy

Duck does. Then we nip off for a quick hot-stone massage and face pack.

Then after a quick swim, we go crazy with an excursion to a medieval church or, even more extreme, a monastery, where we stitch the groom up, good and proper, by forcing him to ring the evensong bells with hilarious consequences.

Finally, after tea, we have an evening at a health farm where we drink wheat-grass, bathe in mud and have our nails done for no other reason than to take revenge on the idiot of the group, who would hate it and on his eventual arrival back home when asked, 'Did you have a nice time?' will have to say, 'No,' holding up his hands. 'No, I had a terrible time, look at my hands. My skin is glowing, I feel radiant and worst of all I can remember everything!'

Addendum:
Since writing this I have been on a stag do where everyone was over thirty. We went to Soho. Immediately images will have come into your head. Banish them. The most hedonistic thing we did was to have a *tarte au citron* and espresso at Patisserie Valerie. Later that night we were refused entry to a Rock & Roll bar for being too smart.

The revolution has started. I'm off to march on Parliament – who's in?

Health Food Shops

I try to live a healthy lifestyle. I swim and go to the gym and watch what I eat and while I wouldn't say I *frequent* my local health food shop, I do pop in from time to time. It's where I go to get the bags of dried lentils I never use, sesame seed crispbreads I never eat and the organic ginger cordial I never drink. I don't know why I buy them, to be honest. I think it's just in case there's a flash-flood and a hippy gets trapped in my house.

The other reason I like to go to my health food shop is for 'health-off-the-shelf'. I like to believe that there are short cuts to health. I've got a weakness for doughnuts and I have at times been known to maim for a slice of Battenberg, but I do also like the idea of the super-food. I want to believe that if you eat enough broccoli it can make you live for ever or at the very least stop you making a loud groan every time you get out of a chair. Even better, I like to think that by eating super-foods you actually can assume superpowers, although I appreciate that they might not be as useful as Superman's:

'Hi, Wheat-grass Man?'

'Yes, sir.'

'Are you here for the new superhero interviews?'

'Yes sir, thank you, sir.'

'OK, what is it you do?'

'At moments of crisis I have the power to make everyone feel like they've had a load of grass shoved in their mouth.'

'Right, and who exactly does this help?'

'Sir, people who like the taste of grass in… er… a time of crisis, sir!'

'No one likes the taste of grass, ever.'

'Sir, maybe I could do hay-fever aversion therapy, sir?'

'OK, well thanks for coming, we'll be in touch.'

'Yes sir, thank you, sir.'

'Next? Hi, what's your name?'

'I'm Green Tea Man.'

'OK, what's your special power?'

'I arrive at restaurants in the nick of time and give everyone a really disappointing end to their meal.'

'Right, so say, for example, there was an asteroid hurtling towards Earth. How would you react?'

'I would work out the exact location of impact, rush over there, then arrive at the restaurant nearest the point of impact... and give everyone a really disappointing end to their meal.'

'Right. Not the most adaptable superpower of all time, then?'

'No, it is pretty specific.'

'OK, thank you, we'll be in touch. Next?'

'Hello, I'm Soya Milk Girl.'

'Well hello, Soya Milk Girl! At last someone with some sophistication and class.'

'Thank you.'

'You wouldn't believe the freaks I've just had in here.'

'I can imagine.'

'So what's your special power?'

'I lactate soya milk.'

'Get out. Next!'

'Ah hello, what's your name?'

'Bean Sprouts Boy.'

'Right, and what is it you do?'

'I arrive at your house with enough bean sprouts for two stir-fries, only offer enough bean sprouts for one stir-fry, then use my superpowers to sit in your fridge under a half-peeled-back film lid until I go brown.'

'That's not a superpower.'

'I know.'

'Get out.' (ON PHONE TO RECEPTIONIST) 'Sarah, this isn't going well. How many more have we out there? Two? OK, send the next one in, please. Hello, what's your name?'

'I'm Alfalfa Man.'

'OK, and what's alfalfa?'

'Not sure.'

'What?'

'Dunno. No one really knows.'

'What do you mean, "no one really knows"?'

'Well… alfalfa! What is it? It just sounds like the noise you'd make if someone shoved grass in your mouth.'

'Don't you start. So you don't know what you are?'

'Absolutely no idea. Out?'

'Yes, out. Right, next?'

'Hello, you look normal. What's your name?'

'Geoff.'

'Forgive me, Geoff, that's not a very superhero sort of name.'

'Er, no, I haven't got any superpowers myself, but I've got a bag of superpower pills.'

'OK, what are they made of?'

'Dead bits of Dr Gillian McKeith.'

'They're what?'

'Dead bits of Dr Gillian McKeith, you know, from the *You Are What You Eat* programme on the telly.'

'Yes, I know who she is. That wasn't the bit I was questioning. Did you say *dead bits* of her?'

'Yes, you know, toenails, hair, the area behind her eyes, her love of life, you know the sort of thing. We chuck it into a machine that turns it into pills that give you a superpower.'

'OK, and what is the superpower?'

'They make you believe that sifting through other people's poo is perfectly normal behaviour.'

'You've got five seconds to convince me not to say the word "out".'

'Um... the first batch of pills comes with a free sluice and nose clip?'

'OUT.' (TO RECEPTIONIST) 'Sarah, hi. I resign.'

So my attitude to super-foods at the moment is mixed, as exemplified by my current fad, manuka honey. It's a super-food that, apparently, is amazing for your immune system and is particularly good at fighting colds. At twelve quid a jar, that should be the least it can do. For that kind of money it should be able to grow back a limb, cure Alzheimer's and sit in for your GP during the summer. I enjoy taking it and I believe it's doing me good, but actually if I stop and think about it, it's probably just honey. I mean, it can't be *that* amazing, can it? It's just honey made in New Zealand from the manuka tree. If it is so amazing then why haven't the bees that collect it got super-powers? They don't just put it on their toast; they're covered in it all day long. But if you look at the bee on the side of the jar, he's not even wearing a cape. In fact, he looks a bit grumpy. No surprise, really, when you think about it. It must get a bit tedious only being allowed to get pollen from one tree.

'All right, Steve? What did you do today?'

'All right, Jarred? I went to the manuka tree and collected pollen.'

'And I did! Got any plans for the weekend?'

'Yeah, I thought I'd go to the manuka tree and collect pollen.'

'No way! Me too, might see you down there. Hey, what are you doing for your holidays this year?'

'Oh, me and the family are going to try to get away.'

'Oh yeah, where to?'

'Oh, we're probably going to go to the manuka tree and collect pollen.'

'Jesus, Steve, have you ever felt life hasn't panned out the way you thought it would?'

How can they possibly claim that the honey is only made from pollen from one tree? They stop bees wandering off? You can't put a bee on a lead. They must pick up pollen from other plants, even if it's just when they have a sit-down for a rest.

If my scepticism ended here, I could be happy eating my breakfast, imagining that at best I was getting superpowers, and at worst that I was just eating expensive but very tasty toast. But there is something else.

These days image matters, especially in advertising. There's a reason that George Clooney advertises espressos, Keira Knightly advertises perfume and Jeremy Kyle doesn't advertise anything. So here's a thing: how come people who work in health food shops often look really ill?

My problem is that the bloke who works in my health food shop looks so unhealthy, he's like an anti-advert. I reckon when he is in peak condition he is, at best, a bit under the weather. In an *X Factor – Looking Sickly* series he would storm the auditions and quickly become one of the favourites for boot camp. He's got everything: eczema, asthma, dry cough, long lank hair, baldness, conjunctivitis, halitosis, athlete's foot, chafing, sweat-rash, heat-rash, a constant cold, verrucas, irritable bowel syndrome, scurvy, piles and thrush. OK, some of those I can't prove, but he looks pretty ill. Yet this is the man who is selling me health. Each time I go in now, I worry that what I'm buying isn't going to do me any good at all. My faith is at its weakest when, in cash-till small talk, I ask him if the stuff I'm buying is any good and he says, 'Yes, it's brilliant. I take that.'

I immediately want to put it back on the shelf, ask him for a list of products he regularly takes, and then not buy any of them. That's what happens when the bloke selling you health looks so brittle that you could actually scrumple him into a ball. You do start to wonder if you are wasting your money. All that keeps me going is the thought that maybe the stuff he takes is so good that it's the only thing keeping him alive. I mean, imagine what he would look like if he *wasn't* taking this stuff! He'd probably be so sickly he wouldn't have the energy to put his crystals on. As such, I intend to keep the faith and remain a believer in health foods. There are worse things I could waste my money on, like beer, fags and the *Daily Mail*. However, if I start developing illnesses that I didn't have before, like the ones the bloke has, then I am going to blame him. I'll be up there like a shot to give him a piece of my mind. Unless of course I develop asthma, in which case, in order to avoid a breathless confrontation, I might send him a stern letter.

I Love Sian Lloyd

You got to love Sian Lloyd. I love the way she brings a bit of show biz to the weather. Who'd have thought it was possible to make the weather sexy? Certainly not Derek Brockway, and nor would he claim to. Derek is charmingly conventional with a glint in his eye and the odd gesture with his elbow. You know what you are getting from him: no-frills weather with a smile. Oh, he's a demon when he's walking. Apparently outside of the weather studio there's no holding him back.

'Anyone seen Derek?'

'Sorry, he's already gone.'

'Where to?'

'Walking.'

'Hey Derek, you going to London for the BAFTAs?'

'Sure am.'

'How're you getting there?'

'Very funny, Chris, now pass me my rucksack.'

But with Sian it's different. She's all big red lips, hair in a perfect bob and magic fingers. Derek tells you how it's going to be, Sian *reveals* it like it's a dove from a velvet curtain. If the weather is a magician, she is his glamorous assistant.

'Hello,' she'll say, all sexy, 'here's the weather.' Inside her head you know she lets out a sultry 'mmmmmmm'.

'Oh, Siani! You cheeky minx, weather me up, baby!'

'If we look at the map,' she'll tease, 'you can see a warm front drifting in from the Atlantic...'

'Oh, she liked that!'

'... mmmmmmm!' she'll stifle.

'Sian Lloyd, you are sex on isobars and no mistake.' I think I've worked out why. That thing she's holding in her hand, with the button and the wire attached, it's got nothing to do with the weather. Battery-operated love eggs are what she's got there.

'So,' she'll mew, 'looking ahead to tomorrow there'll be some rain drifting in from the north...' (BUZZ) 'MmnmMMMMMM!' she'll internally squeal! 'And as for the weekend...'

'Oh yes, Siani! What's it going to be like?

Am I going to need something? Something for the weekend, sir?'

She's looking right down the camera now. Oh yes, things are hotting up.

'What's it going to be like, Sian? Tell me!'

'… look out for some amazing *cumulus* clouds…' (BUZZ) '… MMMMMMMMMMMM!'

'Ohhhh, Siani!! You naughty meteorologist!' Did she really just put the little finger of innocence next to her big red lips? Yes she did!

'And winds strong enough…' she pants.

'Go on, Sian!'

'… strong enough…'

'Yes, Sian, I'm right there with you!'

'… winds strong enough to BLOW ALL YOUR CLOTHES OFF!' (BUZZ) 'OHHHHHHHH, YES SIAN, YEEEESSSSSSSSSSSSSSSSSSSSSSSS!'

'MMMMMMMMMMMMMMMMMMMMM' (BUZZ) 'I'M A METEOROLOGICAL SEX QUEEN! EVERYONE BACK TO MINE FOR A CAR KEYS LOTTERY AND A SLICE OF BATTENBERG!!!'

'Oh Sian, you are barometric filth and no mistake! I've never felt like this about a weather forecaster before. Well, John Kettley once, but I was going through a confusing time. You, Sian Lloyd, are the money…'

(SUDDENLY SHE REGAINS COMPOSURE) 'So, have a lovely day tomorrow and a very good night to you all.'

Fix camera with knowing stare and then one final... (BUZZZZZMMMMMMMMMMM!!!'

Thanks, Sian. And I'm spent.

Up in London

I love London. I lived there for a while and it has a mad, intoxicating, irresistible energy, the like of which I have never experienced elsewhere. It's exhausting and relentless and can chew you up and spit you out too but, basically, it's great.

However, we Welsh people have funny ideas about it and certainly act funny when we are in it. One of my best mates phoned me up before a London weekend once, obsessed with the question of whether it was going to be possible to park. Not *where* we were going to park, but whether it was *possible*. I think he thought that once you get inside the M25 your car gets dragged into London like it's the Death Star and you keep driving around and around, as if on a malfunctioning fairground ride, until, eventually, you run out of petrol and that's where you park. He's probably a bit more of a worrier than most; he also asked if he needed travel insurance, where he could buy a stab vest and if it was true that if you drove the wrong way down a one-way street, you went back in time. He's an extreme example of 'Welsh bloke abroad', but, in fairness, I can understand that faced with a trip to the Big Smoke there is some trepidation, because it *is* different there.

For a start, there's a 24-hour culture. Everything's open all the time, which means you can buy a biscuit any time you want. Now this sounds great, but I'm not sure getting a biscuit *should* be that easy. Not if we are to stop consuming so much in order to save the planet. A biscuit is something you should aspire to. You certainly shouldn't be able to get a bag of six big chocolate chip cookies for 60p in a garage at three in the morning. Also, a 24-hour culture totally buggers up the concept of bedtime.

However, the main thing I couldn't understand when I moved to London was why everyone ran up and down escalators. I grew up in Pontypridd and, as a child, coming to Cardiff for a go on the C&A escalator was a treat. I can remember my gran taking me there as if it were a poor man's Alton Towers. Every visit was the same: a few normal rides, then the 'off-road extreme' ride of running *up* the descending escalator. I can feel the nerves now! When you are nine, there is nothing as scary as the moment you reach the flat bit at the top of a descending escalator. In the 1980s, escalators were viewed as a remarkable feat of engineering and something to be admired. Therefore, running up and down them when they were going in your direction anyway made no sense to me whatsoever. Apart from missing out on the ride, you didn't *really* gain that much time. All you got was a bit sweaty.

The other thing I couldn't believe was how impatient people were. For example, on the London Underground the trains come along every couple of minutes. I'll repeat that: 'every couple of minutes'. Most of the time you'll arrive on the platform and the display will read 'Next train…1 min' and a train will turn up a minute later. However, one of the most extraordinary things I ever saw was when a businessman arrived at a platform where the display read 'Next train… 7 min'. He went berserk! He threw his briefcase to the floor, swore, swung a few air punches, called a homeless person a 'twat' and then ran back out the way he had arrived. It was seven minutes! A minute *less* than Led Zeppelin's 'Stairway to Heaven'. To use another example, about as long as it takes to run a relaxing lavender bubble bath; yet he was as furious as though the display read 'Next train... a day'. This is not uncommon. It seems London commuters can cope with a one, two or even three-minute wait. Four minutes, people tut, but remain cool and look to see if there is a platform seat free. For a five-minute wait people start getting their latest Dan Brown out. Six minutes? People are annoyed but just about remain calm enough to lift the lid of their laptop. Seven minutes? Uh-oh! 'LET BEELZEBUB COME DOWN AND TEAR OUT THE SOULS OF ALL ASSOCIATED WITH TRAINS!'

So it's no wonder we think of London as a different place. For a start, we hold it in some kind of awe because, if you're from Wales, across the bridge is abroad, isn't it? And London is some imaginary place, like Narnia. Growing up in Pontypridd I knew people who thought the only way to get there was on the back of a phoenix. My auntie is a great example of this. She is very 'valleys'. When I'd just started getting into comedy, I overheard a conversation between her and my mum. My mum said, 'Have you heard, Chris is getting into comedy?'

My auntie went, 'Oh no, is he? That's a shame.'

My mum said, 'No, no, up in London!'

My auntie went, 'Ohhhhhhhh!', in the very Welsh valleys undulating way, like she'd just been given a gold-plated tin bath. 'Is he?' she confirmed, completely impressed. I could have been doing anything!

'Have you heard Chris is homeless?'

'Oh no, that's a shame.'

'No, no, up in London.'

'Ohhhhhhhhh!'

'Yes, he's pissing in his own sleeping bag under Waterloo Bridge!'

'Is he really?' My auntie would say in awe. 'He's a clever boy. Of all your children I always said he'd be the one to do well for himself.'

We use the word 'posh' a lot in Wales. Having spent time in London I realise in England the word 'posh' means something very different.

Anything's posh if you're from Wales, isn't it? The basic rule of thumb is 'if it's not broken or covered in shit, it's posh'. Being posh in Wales means, as I saw once, a woman eating a ham salad roll with a knife and fork. I once gave my valleys auntie a tea-towel for Christmas, and when she opened it she said, in that same gold-plated tin bath way, 'Ohhhhhh! There's posh!'

It was indeed a nice tea-towel. It was of Llangollen Railway, a much prized kitchen addition. But it wasn't 'posh'. It wasn't 'smart and fashionable', as the dictionary defines it. If you are going to cook a meal and clean up afterwards, it's pretty much a necessity, isn't it? A basic requirement, maybe even 'stock'. I mean, God knows what she *had* been using all those years to dry the dishes. My moment of pleasure in giving a present that someone liked was lost in an image of her using bits of leftover carpet or old pairs of knickers.

The truth is, it's a doddle being posh in Wales. My advice to any English person struggling to make the grade is to skip across the border. A £5.40 toll is a cheap way to gentrify. In England it's a whole different ball game. You have to do all sorts to be posh. You have to wear a cravat, live in a marquee, go to work on a pony. In Wales, a brand-new pair of slip-ons from Shoefayre is posh!

One of my funniest experiences while living in London was in an Ann Summers shop. I don't suppose that's unusual. If you don't find a ball-gag intrinsically hilarious you either have no sense of humour or you are a massive pervert and probably consider a gimp-mask an evening option. The first thing that tickled me as I walked in was the shelves of 'pleasure gels' that lined the walls. You know the sort of stuff, little pots of 'Raspberry Willy Rub' and 'Cherry Clitty-Lick' and other such names for what was essentially melted Pick-and-Mix gloop. However, what was really funny was that on every shelf was a 'Tester'! Now, as seasoned consumers, we are taught that if you are to invest in a product, you should always test it. You should always take a car for a drive and you should always try on a pair of trainers in a shop. Quite how you try out 'Raspberry Willy Rub' without getting arrested, I'll never know.

Anyway, I was there doing genuine research for a film script (no, not that sort of film), and I overheard a conversation. A couple had walked in and the bloke, in the broadest valleys accent, said, 'Oh, there it is! I can see it!'

And his girlfriend went, 'Sshhhhh, mun. Quiet!'

'No, come on, mun,' he said, 'we've been wandering around for twenty minutes. There it is, that's want you want. Butt plug!'

She was scarlet with embarrassment.

'SSHHH! Shut up, mun,' she said, 'people are listening!'

At which point, unable to resist, I turned

around and said, 'I tell you what, that is the funniest conversation I have ever heard!'

With a big smile, he said something only a Welshman who has just met another Welshman abroad would say: 'Ohhhh, where you from?'

'Pontypridd,' I said.

'Never,' he said. 'I'm from Neath.'

Then he reached over me, plucked the butt plug off the shelf, turned to his girlfriend and said, 'Right, are we going to buy this arse thing or what?' And off they went to the till.

Being practical is a very Welsh trait, I think, born of our industrial past. You could see his mindset was 'get it done': get in there, locate sex toy, bond with fellow Welshman, buy sex toy, find a bar. More worryingly, especially for his girlfriend, was that he almost certainly was like that wherever he was or whatever he was doing. On arriving back at their hotel, I'd venture his romantic foreplay mindset was similar: get in there, locate sex toy, get naked, shove toy up girlfriend's arse, get conkers deep, find bar. Ideally, I'm sure that during the process, he'd have liked to have 'bonded with fellow Welshman' too, but even blokes from Neath know where the line is.

I was just grateful that on the way to the till

he didn't catch sight of the shelves of pleasure-gel 'Testers'. Otherwise, what might have occurred would have been less an embarrassing moment and more a diplomatic incident.

No Logo

I'm into the idea of global justice. The World Development Movement, of which I am a member, often arranges conferences which feature key speakers of the Global Justice Movement, and they are brilliantly informative, totally inspirational and sometimes quite funny.

I went to one such event where Naomi Klein was the special guest. In case you haven't read Naomi Klein's book *No Logo*, basically she argues that big corporations and big brands are bad news because they have discovered that the biggest profits are made not by *selling* a pair of trainers but actually by selling a *branded lifestyle* that people adopt as their identity. In other words, if you buy a whole load of Nike gear, for example, you become a walking advert for a corporation that often makes their products in 'sweat-shops' abroad.

'Ideally,' she said in her speech, 'you should seek out non-branded clothes and wear them.'

Well, that's easier said than done, I thought

to myself. I agreed with her but didn't think that was very practical. Where do you get non-branded stuff? Isn't *everything* branded? Then someone asked her about this and her reply was that there existed certain worker-friendly brands from whom it was OK to buy clothes but that where possible you should try to get your clothes in charity shops.

That's all well and good, I thought, after all, no one with any sense of justice would agree that it was OK for us to have cheap branded clothes made by seven-year-olds in Indonesia. Trouble was, I was sitting there in a rather nice pair of Levi Twists, which were all the rage at the time, and a pair of Adidas trainers, and thus I felt a bit of a hypocrite. So at the end of the conference I went to speak to her. As you would expect, she was surrounded by people wanting to do the same, but I waited my turn.

I put it to her that it was hard to avoid wearing brands as they are the ones that make the cool or, more importantly, quality clothes.

'For example,' I said, 'I go road running, but as yet no ethically produced trainers exist.' A real problem, as you can't do a 10k road run in a pair of Dunlop Flash. Even the short walk to the park would be enough to give you shin-splints in a pair of primary school plimsolls.

'It's a bit like,' I said, 'if you're in town and you really need a coffee. It's hard to avoid going to Costa's or a Starbucks.'

She agreed, but she said it was possible, if you tried (she didn't say how), and that what it all boiled down to in the end was a matter of choice.

'If you knew you were going to want a coffee, when you went to town,' she said, 'you could take a Fair Trade one along with you in a flask.'

'Well, that's true,' I said. What I wanted to say was, 'Yeah, but, come on, Klein, a picnic special from a flask isn't a Mochachino, is it?' However, even in the stubborn mood I was in, I could see that this wasn't a strong moral argument.

The truth was, even though she didn't really have a solution to the trainers conundrum, the longer the conversation went on the more I realised that just because ethical shopping was difficult, this wasn't a reason not to do it. My heart sank as I pictured myself going home that night, putting an entire wardrobe into bin bags, and going into Oxfam the next day in a dressing gown.

If there is a God, what happened next is evidence of him taking pity on me. He knew that I didn't agree with nine-year-olds in Indonesia stitching khaki shorts together for Gap, but he also knew I liked my Twists.

'Man, you just have to do it,' said a bloke's voice from behind me. 'I get all my clothes from charity shops, and they're not branded. You just haven't looked hard enough.'

Brilliant, I thought, a modern man with answers! He's probably got a list of cool, counter-culture shops that stock organic, comfy jeans made by British workers on flexi-time who are paid enough to hold down a mortgage in Surrey. He can be my role model. I will make friends with this man and he will become my ethical guide.

He wasn't.

I turned around and what stood before me was not a vision of inspiration. It was a man who looked as if he'd been dragged backwards through a Blue Peter bring-and-buy sale. To do his appearance proper justice, imagine you went to a fancy dress shop to get an outfit for a party where the theme was children's TV. When asked what sort of thing you wanted, you replied, 'I want to look like Jeffery from *Rainbow* but, if it's possible, I want to look even more of a dick.'

Well, this bloke was wearing what they

would have taken down off the rack. Yellow dungarees, a purple paisley silk shirt, red and white stripy socks and brogues. I was being given ethical fashion advice by a clown in his granddad's shoes.

My first thought was about his employment. What the hell sort of job could a man dressed like that do? Policeman? Teacher? Farmer? Solicitor? Paramedic? Magistrate? Bus driver? No, it couldn't be a job where he met people. Writer? Maybe, but even a writer has to go out to meetings. Watchmaker? Jockey? Philosopher? Boxer? There wasn't a job. Whatever job he *did* do, he spent his entire time inappropriately dressed and therefore, as a role model, he was useless. I was just starting out in stand-up comedy at that point. I couldn't go on stage wearing what he was wearing unless I was going to pull balloons out of my bottom. Oh, wait... OK, so there was *one* job he could do.

He meant well and ethically he was as clean as a whistle. But he looked stupid. I know that is what the fashion industry wants me to think, but I'm sorry, I wasn't prepared to dress up like Mr Tumble and spend the rest of my life getting happy-slapped by hoodies. It just wasn't practical.

To explain this to him would have only ended in me offending him. Not deliberately, you understand. I just think it would have been impossible to present my side of the argument without eventually saying, 'Listen, mate, at the end of the day, you look like a twat.'

So I thanked him for his advice and wandered off. As I went I took the glint in Naomi Klein's eye to mean that this bloke wasn't her prime example of how to convince the ethical consumer either. In fact, I'm pretty sure that she was thinking what I was thinking. From that point, therefore, I decided I would continue to support ethical shopping as long as it didn't make me look like a twat.

On the way out of the conference room, I thought I'd have a look at a few of the stalls in the hallway. There was always the same sort of stuff at all these events: Fair Trade chocolate, ponchos, *Lonely Planet* guides to Columbia, dried bananas from Cambodia, etc. Before I tell you what happened next, bear in mind for a moment the sort of people that attend these conferences. Nice people. Nice people who are interested in ending global poverty. A mixture of old hippies, crusties, socialist lecturers, etc. Good selfless people with good selfless hearts.

The sort of people who put 'People before Profit' and who you'd imagine would regularly use the phrase 'after you'. Or so I thought.

It was nearly time for the event to end when one stallholder suddenly shouted out that he was slashing all his stock to half price. The result was that one minute I was casually browsing a particularly nice set of Peruvian pan pipes and the next I was being violently elbowed out of the way by a hippy like a valleys girl at a Primark sale. Pow! He was in, scooped up the pan pipes, slammed his money down in the tobacco-tin till and was gone, off on a crazed quest for other ethical bargains.

On my way home I had a comforting thought. It occurred to me that the bargain-hunting hippy and I had a lot in common. My contact with him was a bit like my experience of talking to Naomi Klein about my Levi jeans. No one's perfect. People are only ever constructs of their time. A hippy still has money and still has to go shopping, and I have to wear trousers in public. Both of us want global justice. It's just that you can't do it instantly, and in the meantime he needed a set of cheap pan pipes and I needed to avoid getting laughed off stage for wearing a pair of prison-issue jeans.

Life, I thought to myself as I strolled along past Parliament, is always a lot more complicated than you think and things are always much harder to achieve than you imagine but, I concluded, this doesn't mean you shouldn't try to do what's right.

As long as, I reminded myself, it doesn't make you look like a twat.

Quick Reads

Books in the Quick Reads series

Quick Reads

We Won the Lottery
Real Life Winner Stories
Danny Buckland

Accent Press

A short, sharp shot of excitement

Fancy cars, big houses and dream holidays are all top of the wish list for the people whose lives are changed by a £1 winning lottery ticket. But what about buying a boob job for your sister or giving away holidays to children with cancer?

For the first time five winners share the details of their shopping sprees. They talk about the highs and lows of their lives after they became millionaires. *We Won the Lottery* also goes behind the scenes at the National Lottery to reveal funny facts, the luckiest numbers, the unusual purchases and exactly what happens when you win.

Quick Reads

Team Calzaghe
Michael Pearlman

Accent Press

A short, sharp shot of excitement

Never beaten in 46 fights, Joe Calzaghe became recognised as one of the greatest sportsmen in British history after his last fight against American great Roy Jones at New York's Madison Square Garden.

The man behind his success is father and mentor Enzo Calzaghe, who has produced four world champions from his tiny south Wales gym.

Team Calzaghe explores the success of the Calzaghe boxing family, which includes Enzo Maccarinelli, Bradley Pryce, Gary Lockett and Gavin Rees.

It also lifts the lid on the boxers' battles with booze, bulimia and the authorities as the Calzaghes defied their critics to rule the boxing world.

Quick Reads

Loose Connections

Rachel Tresize

Accent Press

A short, sharp shot of excitement

Mother-of-two Rosemary is a woman under pressure. With difficult teenaged children, a distant husband and a busy job, the stress is mounting.

The loss of her internet connection pushes her over the edge.

After waiting a month and enduring two failed attempts to fix the problem, a third repair man arrives. When he too says he can't get her back online, his incompetence forces Rosemary to take drastic action.

Soon the repair man realises that Rosemary is not as naive as she first appears. She is a woman with a secret and is capable of causing him harm.

Quick Reads

Inside Out
Real life stories from behind bars

Accent Press

Brought together by their crimes, the prisoners at Parc Prison, Bridgend, share their stories of life on the other side of the security walls.

Whether they are tough criminals or teenagers in trouble for the first time, they all have one thing in common – they had a life outside.

The prisoners have put into words what it's really like doing time at Parc Prison, how they got there and their hopes for the future.

These stories of their lives before crime will surprise and move you, make you laugh and cry in equal measures!

Royalties from this book will go to Parc Prison's arts and educational fund to support creative workshops for prisoners.

Quick Reads

Black-Eyed Devils
Catrin Collier

Accent Press

One look was enough. Amy Watkins and Tom Kelly were in love. But that one look condemned them both.

'Look at Amy again and you'll return to Ireland in a box.' Amy's father is out to kill Tom.

All Tom wants is Amy and a wage that will keep them. But Tonypandy in 1911 is a dangerous place for Irish workers like Tom, who have been brought in to replace the striking miners. The miners drag them from their beds and hang them from lamp posts as a warning to those who would take their jobs.

Frightened for Amy, Tom fights to deny his heart, while Amy dreams of a future with the man she loves. But in a world of hatred, anger and violence, her dream seems impossible until a man they believed to be their enemy offers to help. But, can they trust him with their lives?

Quick Reads

Alive and Kicking
Andy Legg

Accent Press

Andy Legg is one of the best-loved players in Welsh international football and his legendary long throw-in earned him a place in the record book.

One of a select few to play for South Wales arch-rivals Swansea City and Cardiff City, Andy played six times for Wales and more than 600 League games for Swansea, Notts County, Birmingham City, Peterborough, Reading and Cardiff.

But in 2005 his life was turned upside down when a lump in his neck turned out to be cancer. Alive and Kicking is Andy's emotional account of his treatment, his fears for his life and how the messages of support from his fans gave him the strength to fight on and return to the game.

Quick Reads

In at the Deep End
From Barry to Beijing
David Davies

Accent Press

As he was carried off on a stretcher at the Olympics in Beijing, Welsh swimmer David Davies was celebrating his success. He'd won a silver medal in one of the toughest races in the Olympics.

He also won a place in British swimming history as the first male swimmer to win medals at two consecutive Olympic Games in over thirty years.

In At The Deep End: From Barry To Beijing is David's own story of the highs and lows of his career. How a lanky schoolboy from Barry made the swimming world sit up and take notice. From his first success at the Commonwealth Games at the age of 17, he has gone on to win medals at every major championship. And he's still only 24.

About the Author

Chris Corcoran grew up in Pontypridd. A trained teacher, he moved to London where he established himself on the comedy circuit, performing at The Comedy Store and The Glee. He wrote and performed the BBC Radio Wales sit-com *Those That Can't*, with Greg Davies, as well as co-presenting *The Rhod Gilbert Show* with his housemate, Rhod Gilbert. His TV credits include the cult CBeebies children's show *Doodle Do* and Rob Brydon's *Identity Crisis*. He tours with his live stand-up show, regularly performs his live comedy show 'Chris Corcoran's Committee Meeting' and has supported Rob Brydon on tour.